T0147138

THE
BEST
MANDALA
COLORING BOOK

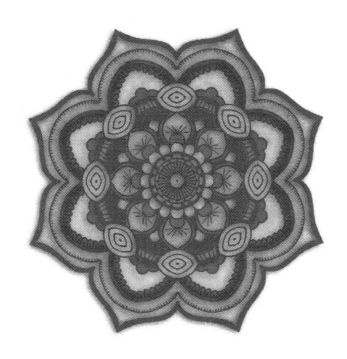

Nyeli Glaser and Dora Vandekamp

BALBOA
PRESS

A DIVISION OF HAY HOUSE

Balboa Press books may be ordered through booksellers or by contacting:

Balboa Press
A Division of Hay House
1663 Liberty Drive
Bloomington, IN 47403
www.balboapress.com
1 (877) 407-4847

ISBN: 978-1-5043-5599-5 (sc)
ISBN: 978-1-5043-5600-8 (e)

Print information available on the last page.

Balboa Press rev. date: 9/01/2016

The Best Mandala Coloring Book features three balancing meditations to relax your mind and help you create beautiful mandalas. If you would like the audio versions of these meditations, register on our website at *www.naurainc.com*. You will receive three guided meditations for free by email. We look forward to meditating with you!

— Dora and Nyeli

INTRODUCTION

Success comes in many forms, but we believe that happiness is a pretty big part of it. With that in mind, we created a coloring book that inspires inner peace, creativity, and abundance. The Best Mandala Coloring Book comes from the knowledge that coloring mandalas can empower you to manage thoughts and feelings on your own. Through the healthful activity of coloring you will practice positive habits to overcome stress and anxiety, reducing negative thoughts, and becoming more naturally and intuitively at ease. This allows for higher energy levels, increased creativity, and bigger successes.

Happy coloring! ☺

Nyeli Glaser

Nyeli Glaser is an experienced art therapist and motivational speaker who helps individuals develop anti-stress techniques through artistic expression. She empowers people to transform by helping them create joy, happiness, and success in all areas of their lives. Nyeli's passion for art and design is influenced by her architectural background, and her art exhibition experience in her native Panama. She now lives in South Florida with her husband Rick and her English Bulldog Conny.

Dora VandeKamp

Dora VandeKamp is a mindfulness expert and wellness writer who helps individuals tap into their own powerful energy, transforming their relationships with others and themselves. A graduate of California State University, Northridge and The Institute for Integrative Nutrition, Dora uses unique strategies to create extraordinary results and has helped many people create the life of their dreams. She lives in South Florida near the beach with her two dogs.

You can find Nyeli and Dora at www.naurainc.com and on social media at @naurainc.

VISUALIZATION MEDITATION

One of the best ways to reach for better feeling thoughts is to visualize fun and exciting experiences.

To start, sit comfortably, in a chair, or on the floor in a cross-legged position. Another option is to lie down on your back, palms facing upwards, and legs hip distance apart.

Relax your face and your jaw, allowing the inside of your mouth to be relaxed.

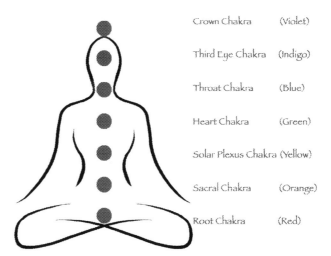

Crown Chakra   (Violet)

Third Eye Chakra   (Indigo)

Throat Chakra   (Blue)

Heart Chakra   (Green)

Solar Plexus Chakra (Yellow)

Sacral Chakra   (Orange)

Root Chakra   (Red)

Choose a place in your mind where you feel most at ease and happy. This may be a tropical beach, your dream home, a lush green forest, or driving along the coast in your dream car.

There are no restrictions as long as it is a safe and inviting place for you. Your place can be anywhere that you choose, whether or not you have been there before.

Visualize yourself in this place as you incorporate all of your senses into your mind. Imagine what this place feels like, maybe there is a cool breeze, or a warm sun. Maybe there is a fragrance or a chorus of birds singing. As you walk, see your feet on the surface of the ground. Observe the environment, feel the temperature, and listen to the surrounding sounds. As you do this, see yourself being relaxed and content. Use your imagination; this does not have to be realistic! You might even see yourself in abundance of money, or of health. Feel the feelings that come to you when you imagine yourself in this place. You might feel joyful, exhilarated, and at peace. Practice this for approximately 8 minutes.

When you are ready, gently bring yourself back to the present moment. Become aware of your surroundings. Feel your body, and allow yourself some time to come back to a present state of mind.

Your imagination is capable of manifesting great things. Have fun!

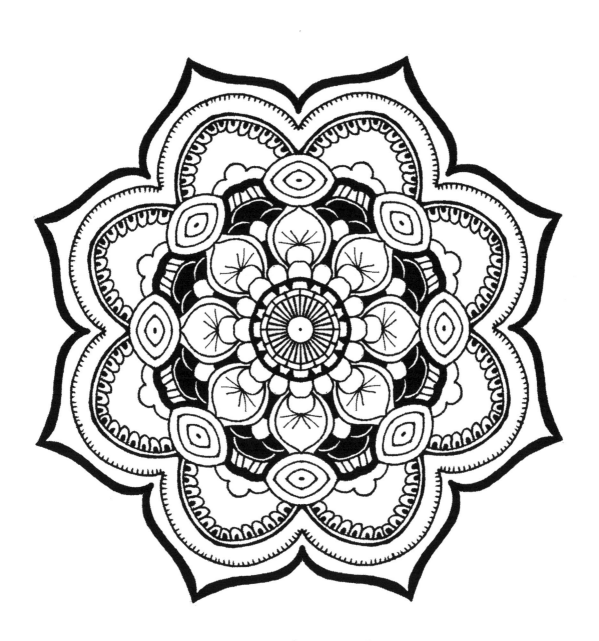

"I am the source of my own happiness."

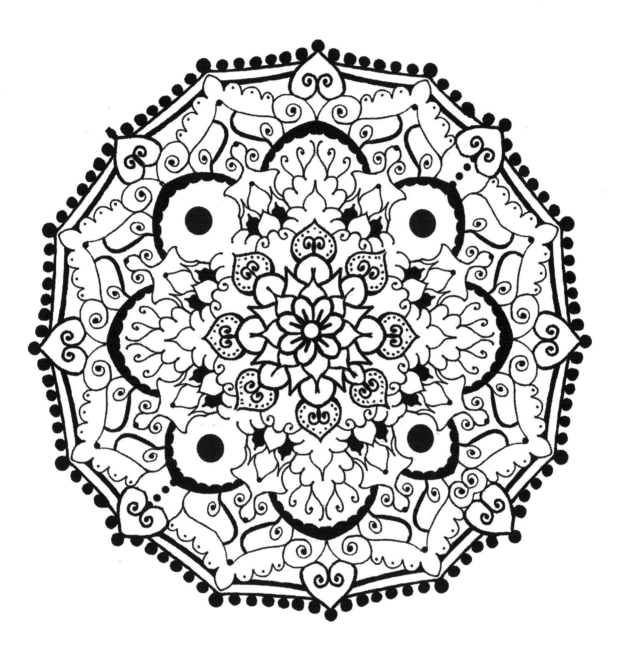

"My thoughts create my experience."

"I came from joy, I am joy."

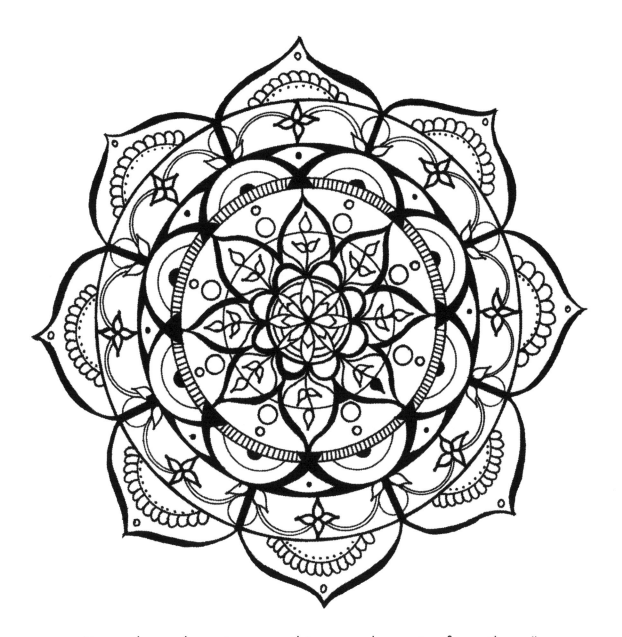

"I am always learning new things, and growing from them."

"I choose happiness, success, and abundance in my life."

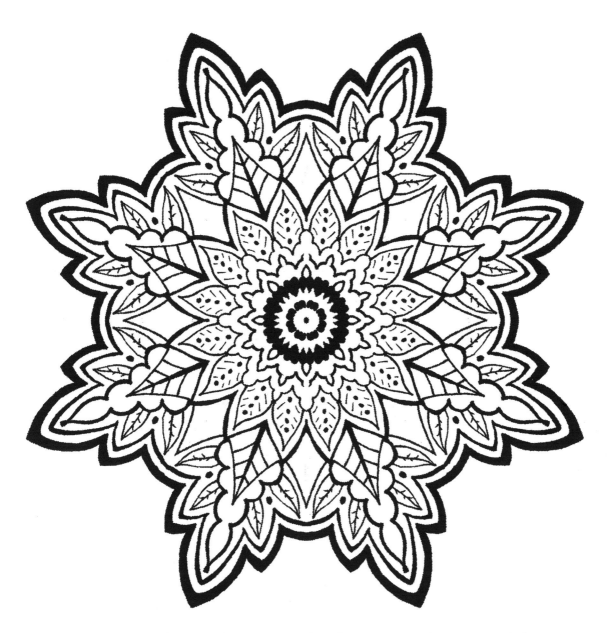

"I possess the qualities I need to be extremely successful."

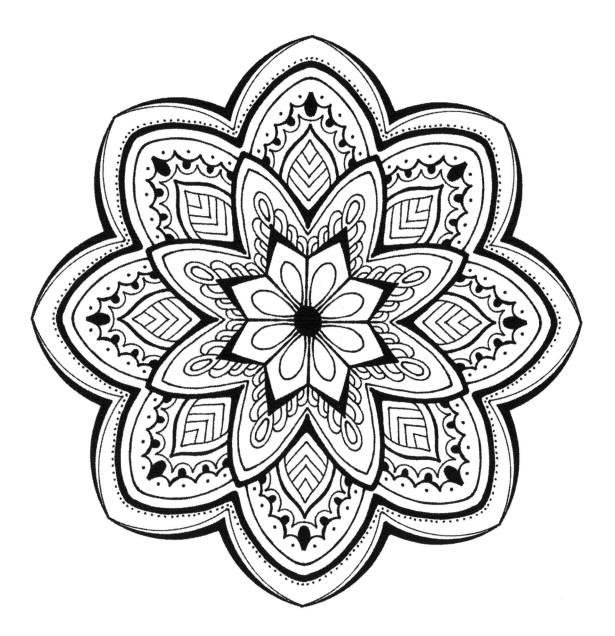

"I love what I have and I am grateful for it."

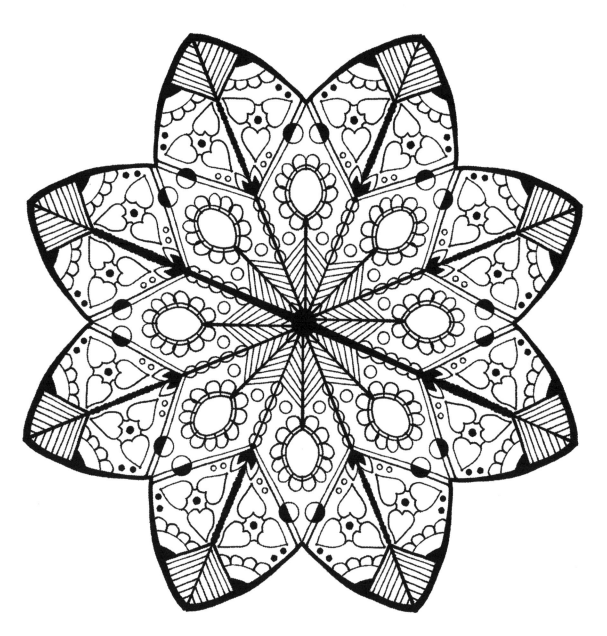

"Creative energy flows through me and leads me to new brilliant ideas."

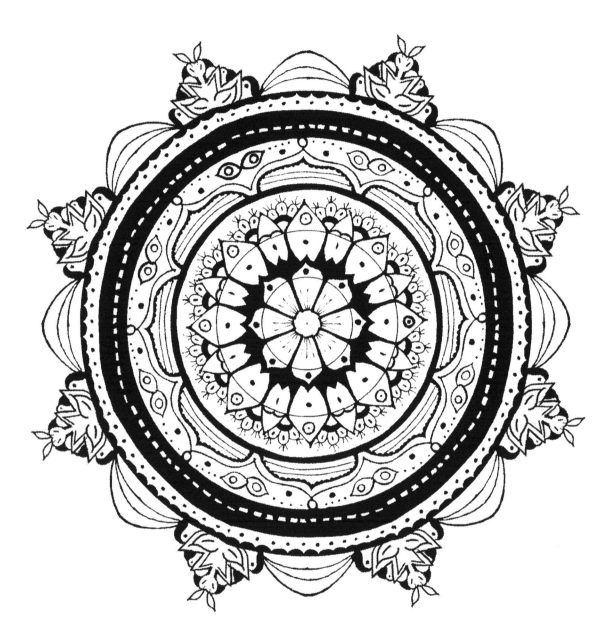

"Beautiful things happen in my life daily."

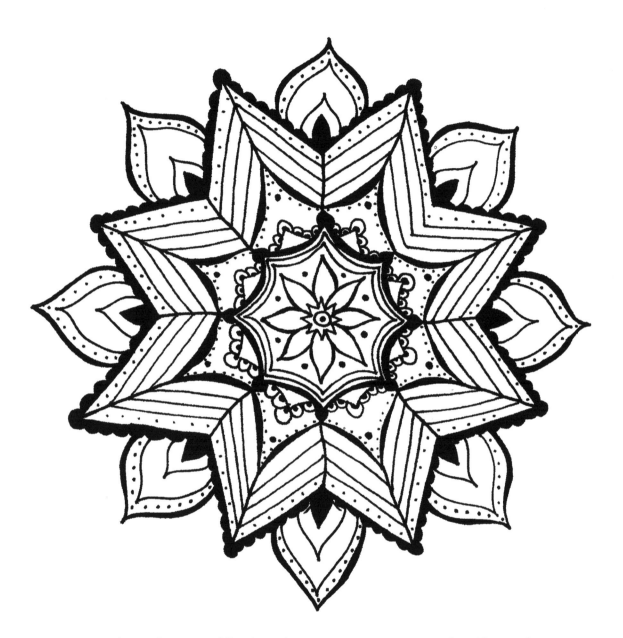

"My thoughts are filled with positive energy and self worth."

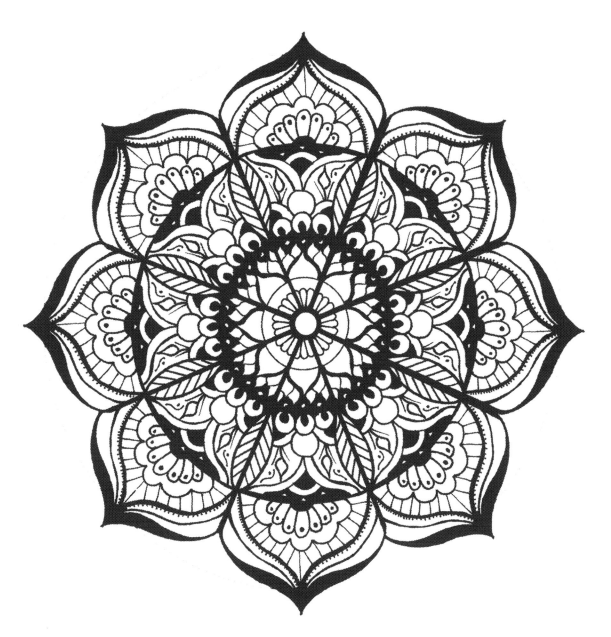

"I keep my thoughts positive because they shape my reality."

ENERGY FLOW MEDITATION

Chakras are the energy centers that affect the physical and energetic harmony of your physiological system. These chakras distribute energy throughout your body. If your chakras become blocked, imbalance occurs. This imbalance affects your physical, emotional and spiritual health in a very significant way. To the right is an illustration with the names, colors, and locations of each chakra.

The lower energy centers are associated with survival, creative tendencies, love, and sense of self. The higher energy centers are associated with spiritual consciousness, communication and intuition.

To open your chakras, spend some time visualizing the colors of each chakra. You can sit in a chair or lay down comfortably. Start at your root chakra, imagining a vibrant red color at the base of your spine. See this color as a glowing red orb that continues to grow brighter and brighter. After several minutes of focusing your attention on this orb, move your attention up to your sacral chakra, slightly below your belly button. Again, envision a radiant orb of light, this time orange in color, growing brighter and brighter. After several minutes, move your focus up to your solar plexus chakra and repeat this method but with yellow. Continue this, as you move up the chakras, using green for your heart chakra, blue for your throat chakra, turquoise for your third eye chakra, and violet for your crown chakra. Take several minutes for each chakra. Then, visualize a white light surrounding your whole body. Take five deep breaths, making sure to release completely each time.

Gently become aware of your surrounding and your body. Allow yourself some time to come to a present state of mind.

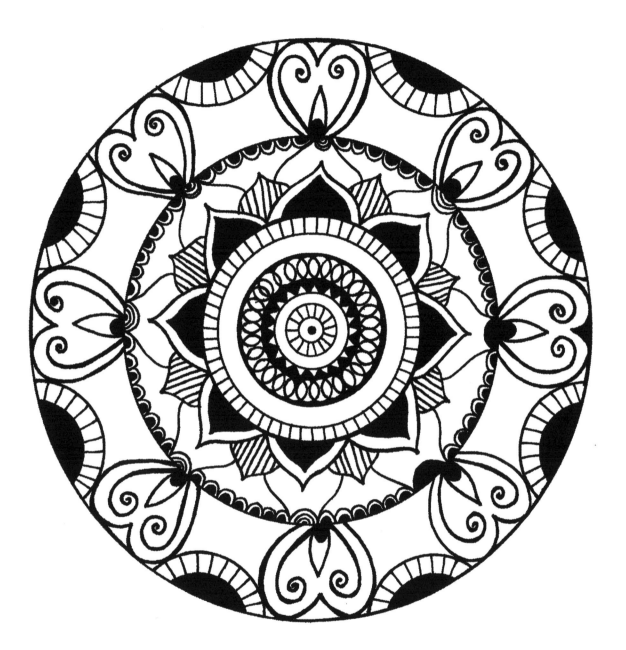

"I enjoy creating opportunities for success."

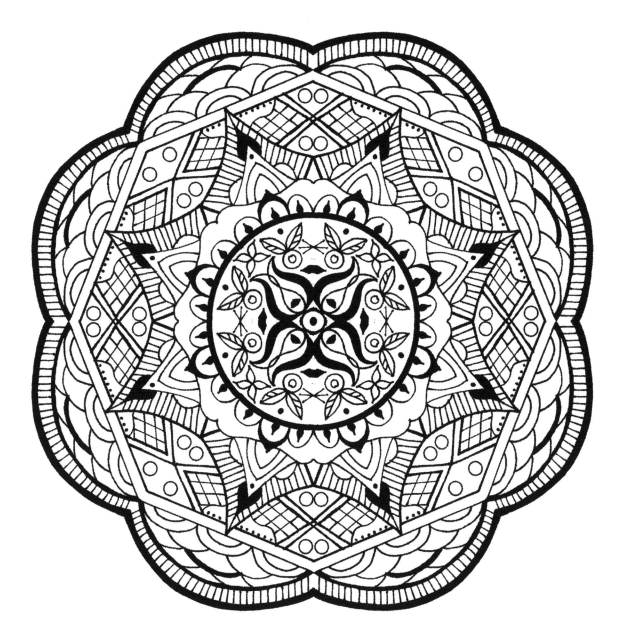

"I radiate love and happiness."

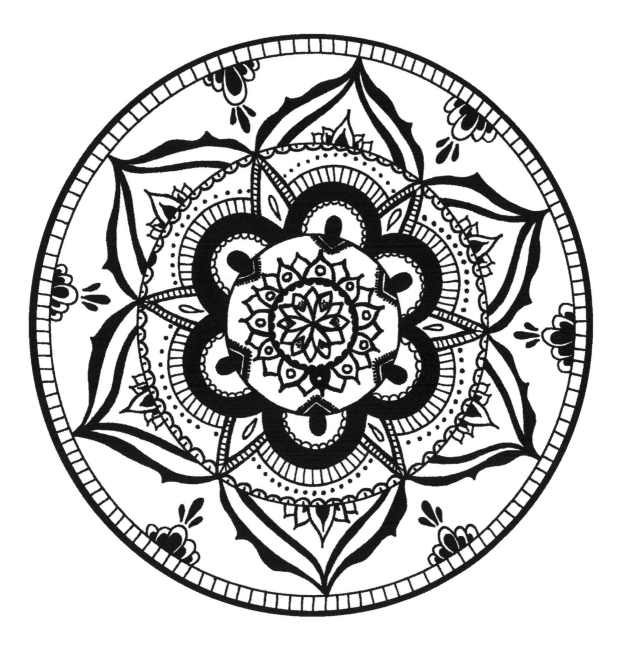

"Money flows to me easily and frequently."

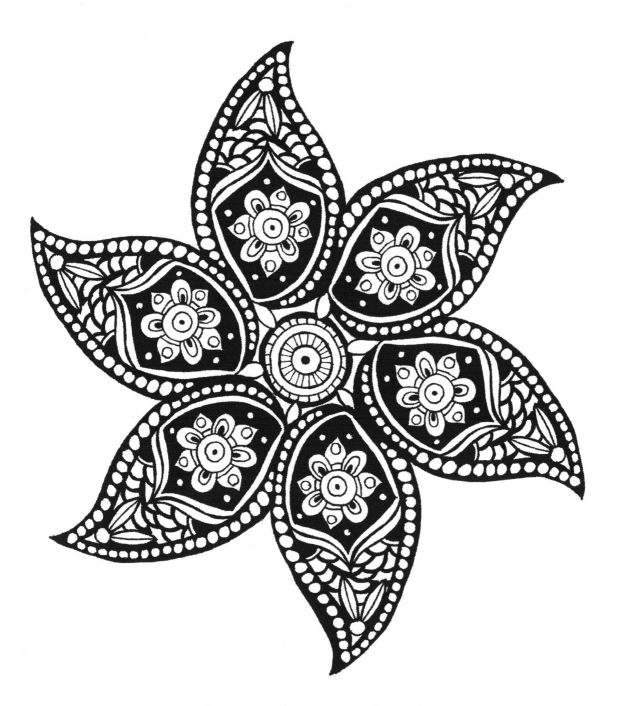

"My life is based on gratitude and joy."

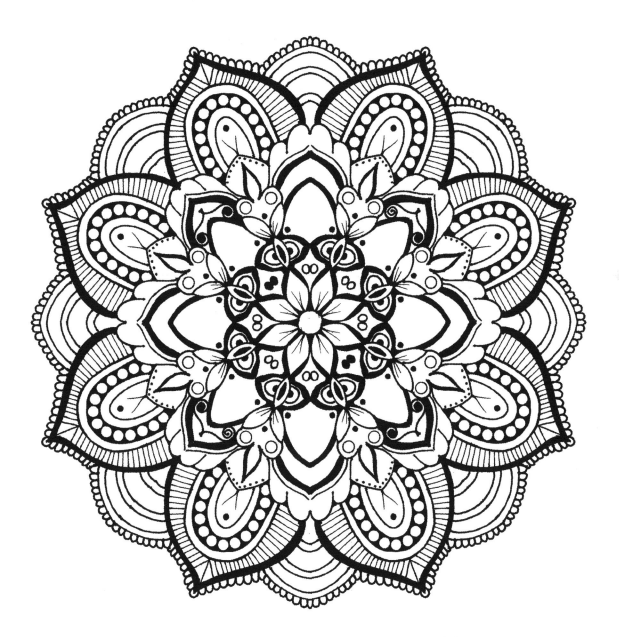

"I am on my way to creating great wealth."

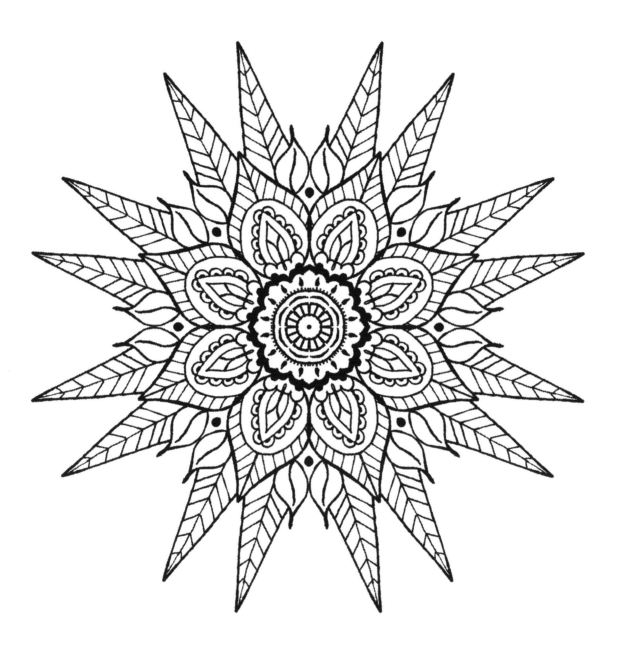

"I surround myself with positive people."

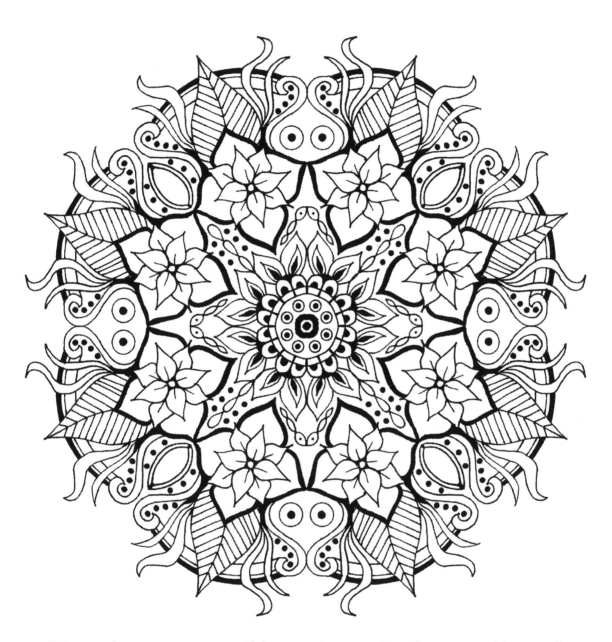

"Every day, in every possible way, I am getting better and better."

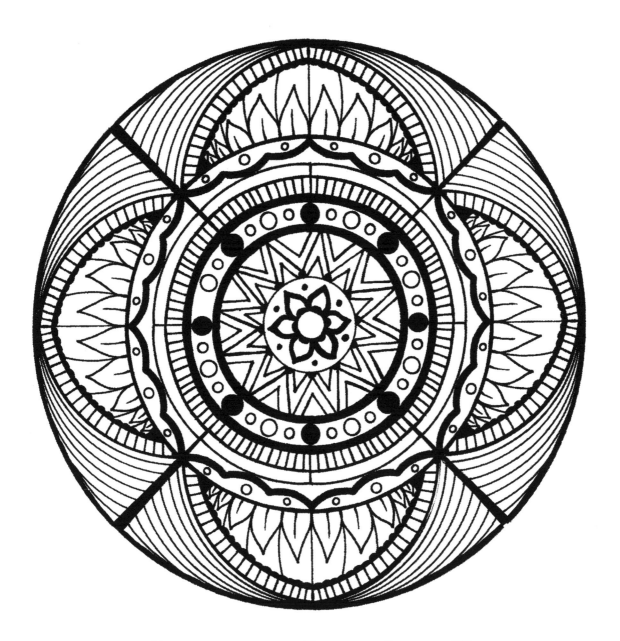

"I create peace and harmony for myself."

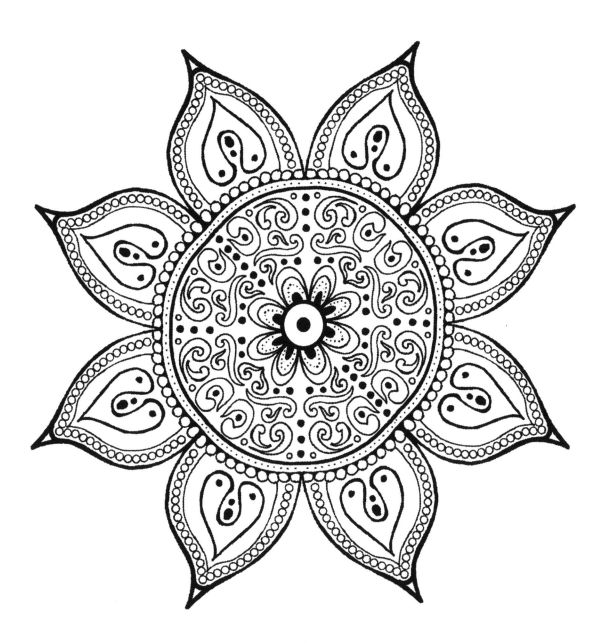

"I am on the path to greatness."

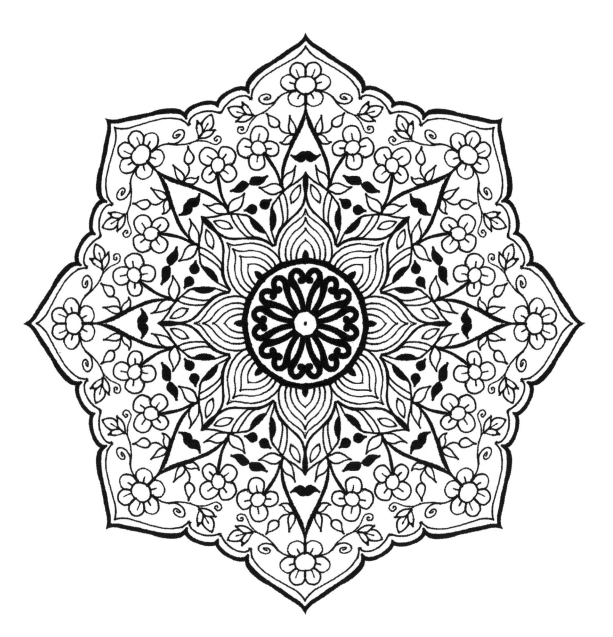

"My happiness depends on what I think."

CREATIVITY MEDITATION

One of the best ways to inspire your creative mind is to stimulate your body's organs. As your blood flow increases, your brain feels a greater sense of focus and positive energy.

Sit comfortably, in a chair, or on the floor in a cross-legged position. Relax your face and your jaw, allowing the inside of your mouth to become relaxed. Imagine that your hands are very heavy, weighing down your arms, pulling your shoulders down and lengthening your arms and neck. Imagine that your legs are being pulled away from you, gently stretching out your thighs and calves, and your torso. As you feel your body stretch, envision that the muscles become long and loose, giving up all tension and relaxing into the ground or chair that you are in.

Inhale deeply, concentrating on the sensation of your breath as it travels through your nose, down through your throat and to your chest. Now, release fully. Repeat this process ten more times, each time focusing on the sensations of the breath and the body. Continue breathing relaxed breaths and notice your body as it becomes free from tension. Notice your feet, and consciously feel them relaxing. In this way, consciously relax your calves and shins, your knees and thighs, and your hips. Notice a pleasant, restful sensation now encompassing your lower body.

Focus now on relaxing your abdomen, stomach and chest. Imagine your spine
and your ribs gently sinking into the floor or chair, feeling your heartbeats. As
you notice the rhythm, you might feel as if your whole body is flowing to the
rhythm of your heartbeat. This is positive energy flowing through you.
Turn your attention to your throat, relaxing the muscles there. Now relax
your facial muscles, and the crown of your head. Feel the sensation
of complete and utter relaxation washing over you, and imagine that
only positive energy is flowing through your entire body.

As you lay or sit, take three deep breaths, allowing the lungs to fill with healing oxygen,
and then releasing each breath fully. Once you have finished with these breaths, take a
few moments to consciously open your mind to any creative thoughts or ideas. When you
are ready, bring yourself to the present moment. Become aware of your surroundings
and your body. Allow yourself some time to come to a present state of mind.

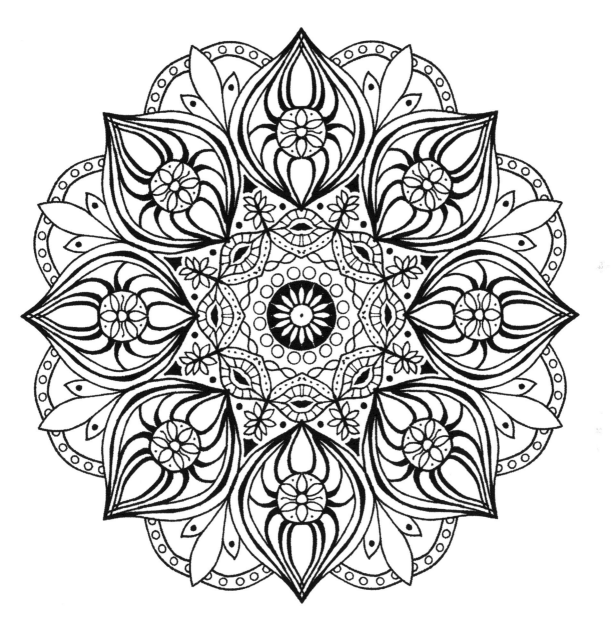

"I love being healthy and feeling good in my body."

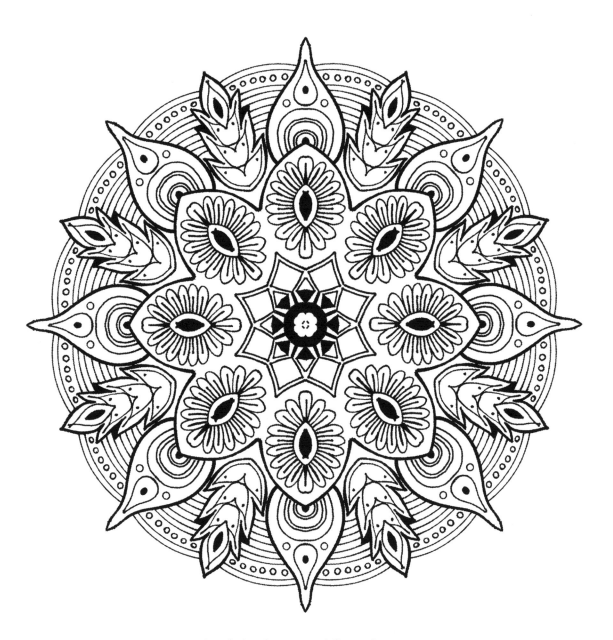

"I am playful, I live my life in happiness."

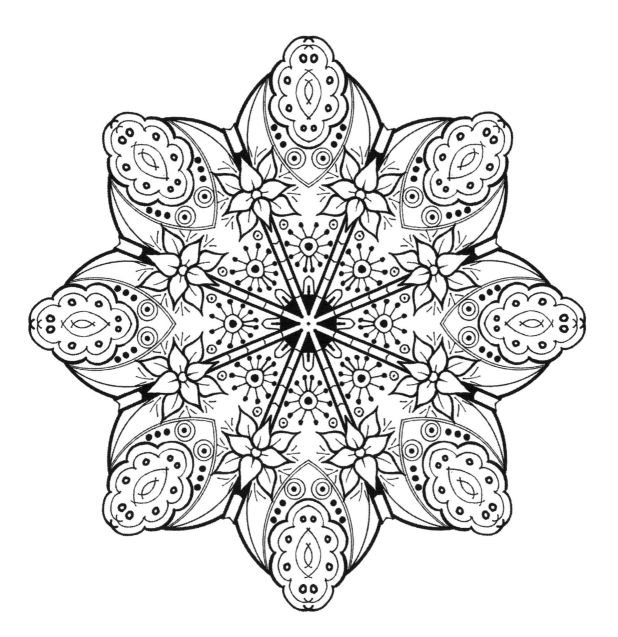

"I am grateful that my body knows how to heal itself in many ways."

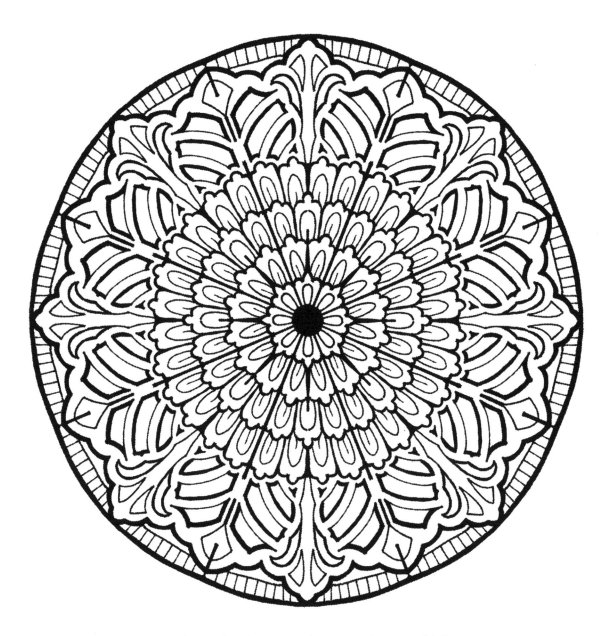

"Today I find joy in the simplicity of life."

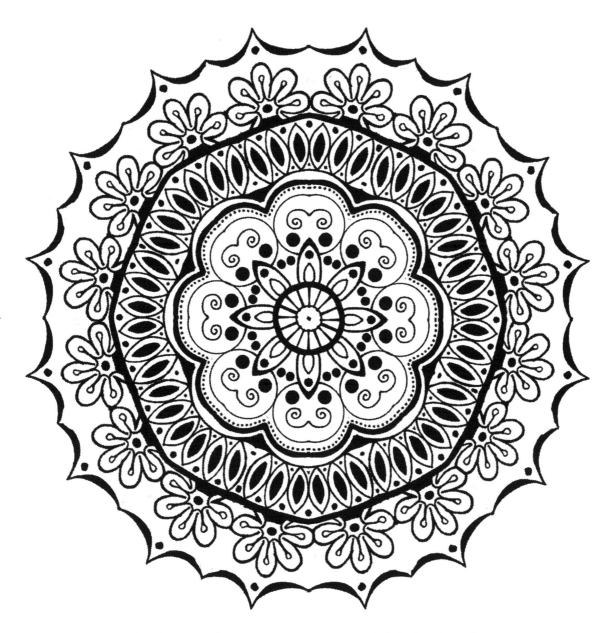

"I feel myself growing more youthful day by day."

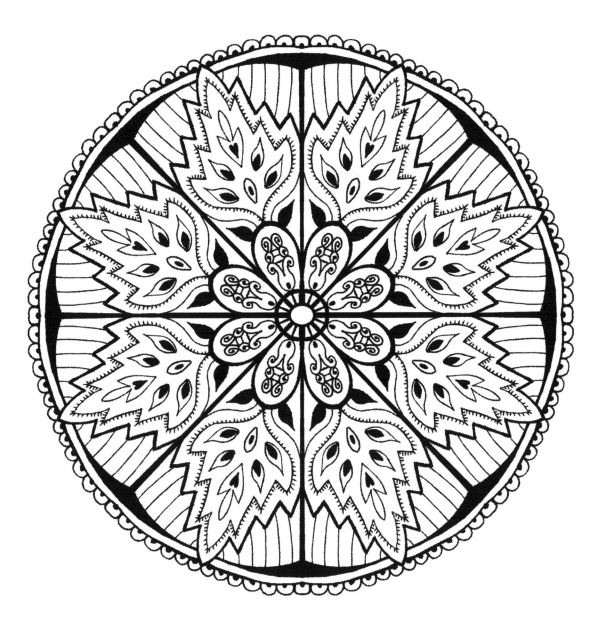

"Everything is getting better every day."

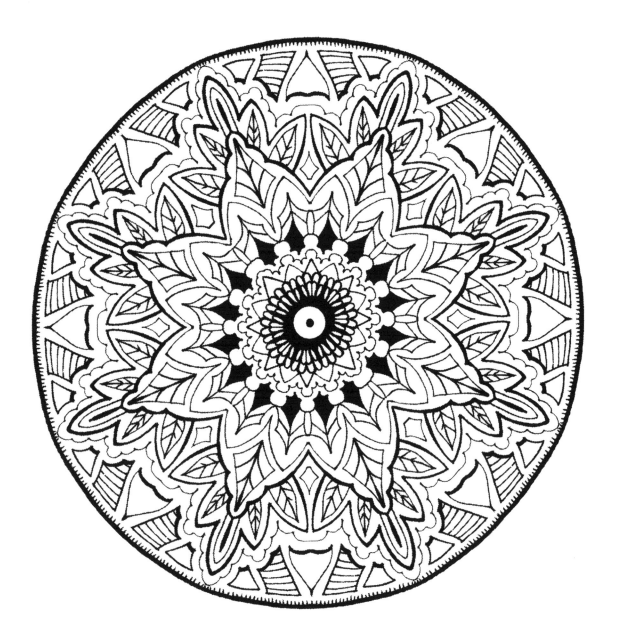

"I have many gifts and talents."

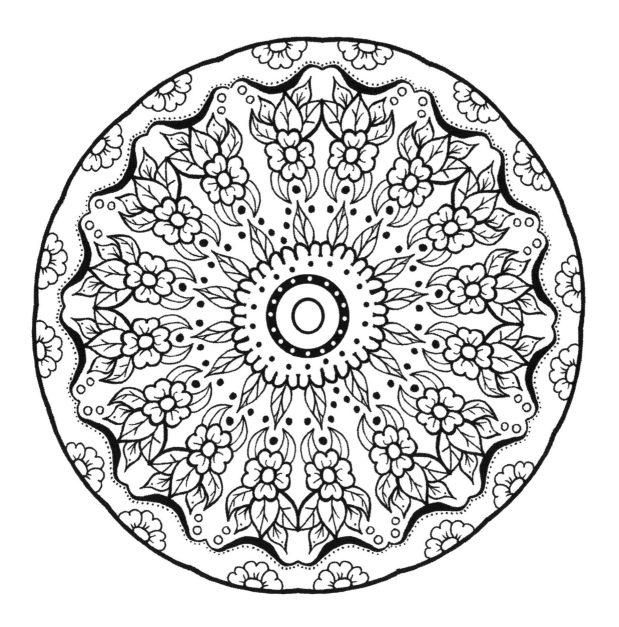

"I release all resistance so I may express my creativity."

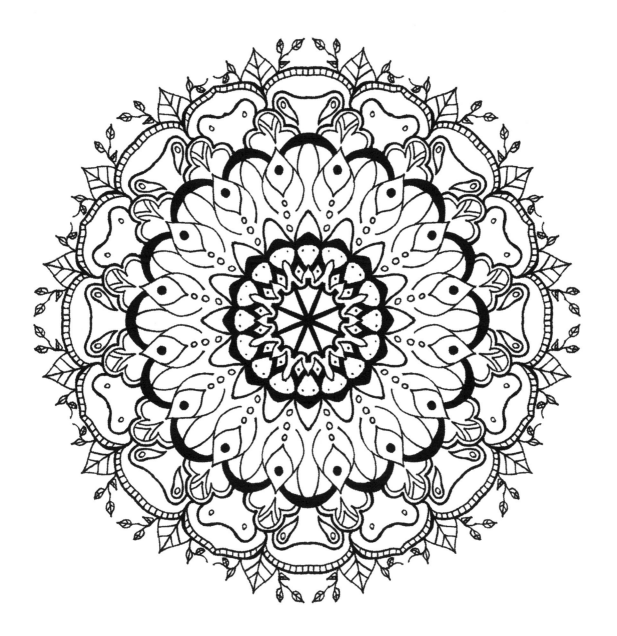

"Through each experience I become more
capable of achieving great things."

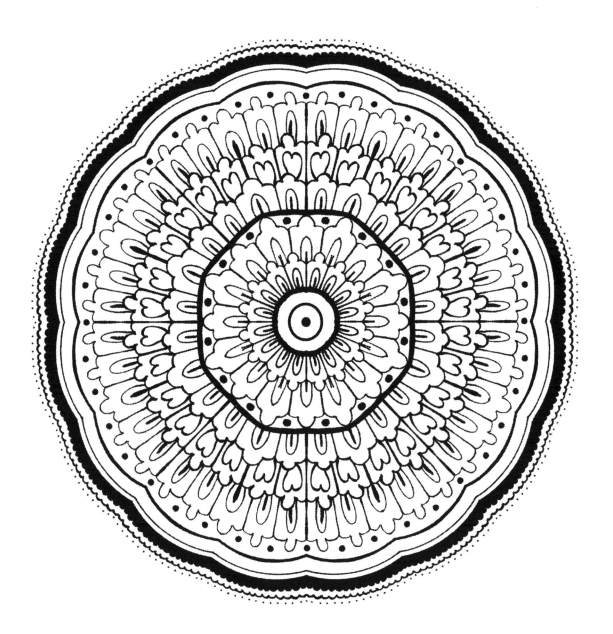

"As I practice gratitude I transform my life."

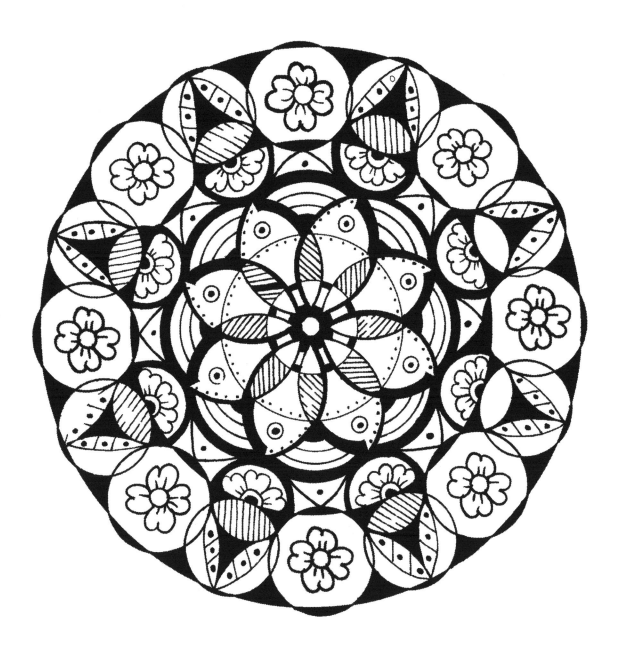

"I am filled with peace and love."

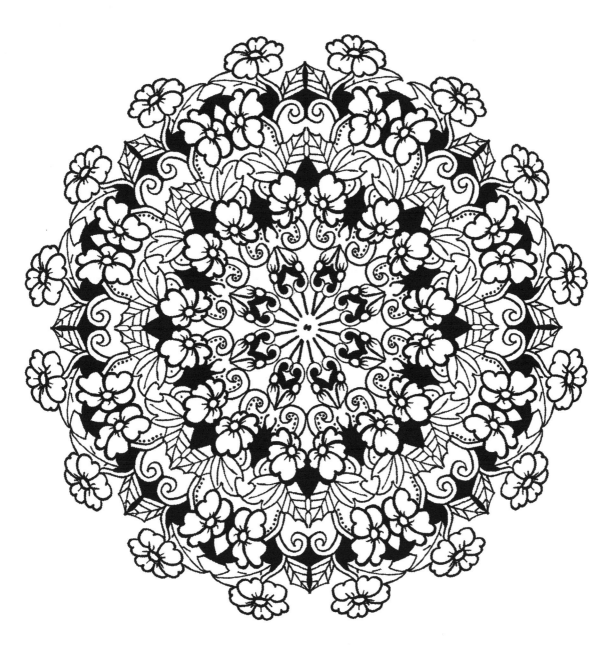

"I choose to feel good in this moment."

Printed in the United States
By Bookmasters